Pencil, Paper, Draw!™

W9-CNA-516

Tonka

STERLING

New York / London
www.sterlingpublishing.com/kids

10 9 8 7 6 5 4 3 2 1

Published by Sterling Publishing Co., Inc.
387 Park Avenue South, New York, NY 10016
Distributed in Canada by Sterling Publishing
c/o Canadian Manda Group, 165 Dufferin Street,
Toronto, Ontario, Canada M6K 3H6
Distributed in the United Kingdom by GMC Distribution Services,
Castle Place, 166 High Street, Lewes, East Sussex, England BN7 1XU
Distributed in Australia by Capricorn Link (Australia) Pty. Ltd.
P.O. Box 704, Windsor, NSW 2756, Australia

Sterling ISBN 978-1-4027-5356-5

For information about custom editions, special sales, premium and
corporate purchases, please contact Sterling Special Sales
Department at 800-805-5489 or specialsales@sterlingpublishing.com.

Contents

Introduction

Drawing is a lot of fun and a great hobby. You can draw alone or with friends. Draw while watching television or quietly in the library at school. Take a pad of paper and some pencils on a long car trip to pass the time. Keep in mind that drawing is just like playing music, sports, or learning state capitals, it takes practice. Don't expect to be great on the first try. You will learn more and more each time you draw. By putting the date on the bottom or back of your drawings, you can keep track of your progress. Hang your drawings up in your room so you can look at them and see what you can improve on. Just have fun drawing and you will see your drawing skills improve each day.

How to Use This Book

You will notice there are different colored lines in each drawing step. Blue lines are the new steps. Black lines are the lines done in a previous step and gray lines are lines not needed in the final drawing.

The blue lines are the new lines to draw.

Black lines are the final lines in the drawing.

The gray lines will need to be erased.

Solid blue areas are going to be filled with black.

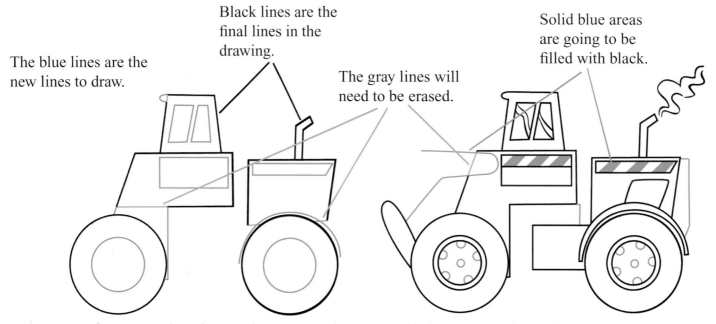

When you first start drawing make sure to draw very light. Many of the shapes and lines you start with are guides and will not be needed in the finished drawing.

You don't need to erase the gray lines in each step as you draw. In the final step press harder with your pencil and trace over the lines you want to keep. You can even go over the final step with a black pen.

A trick that most artists use when drawing is a sheet of tracing paper. Sketch your drawing following the steps in the book. When you are finished lay a sheet of tracing paper over your finished sketch. Now trace over the lines you want to keep in your final drawing.

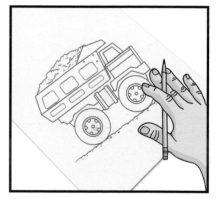

After following the steps in this book try drawing something that's not in this book. You should learn to view animals, people, or machines as a group of many shapes and lines. When you begin to see how simple shapes and lines combine to create form, you will be well on your way to drawing anything you want. I hope you have fun learning to draw, and remember, practice makes perfect.

8

CAUTION
AREA UNDER
CONSTRUCTION

Tonka

11

Construction Workers

Construction workers are the most important people on the scene of a building site. They have to drive the big tough Tonka™ Trucks.

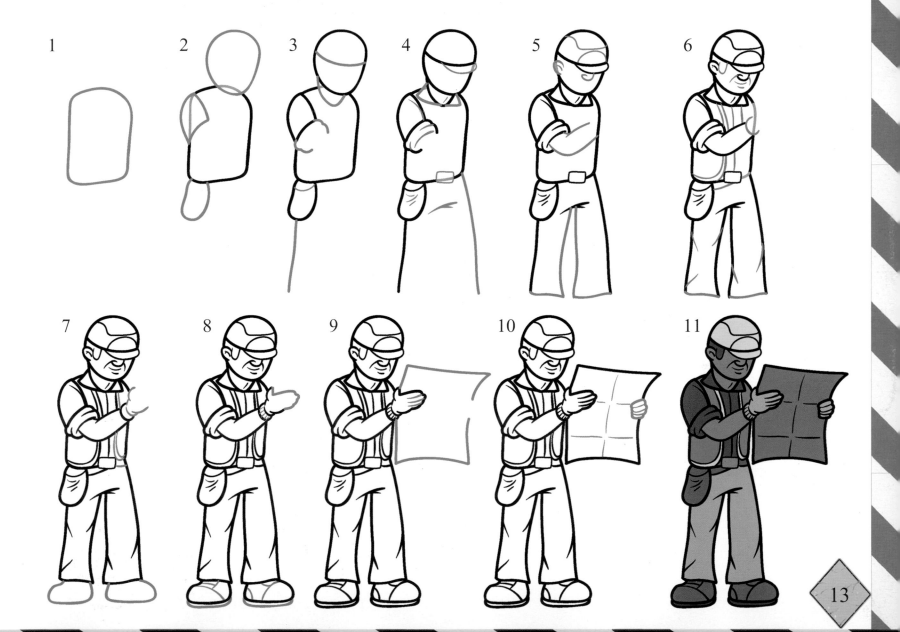

13

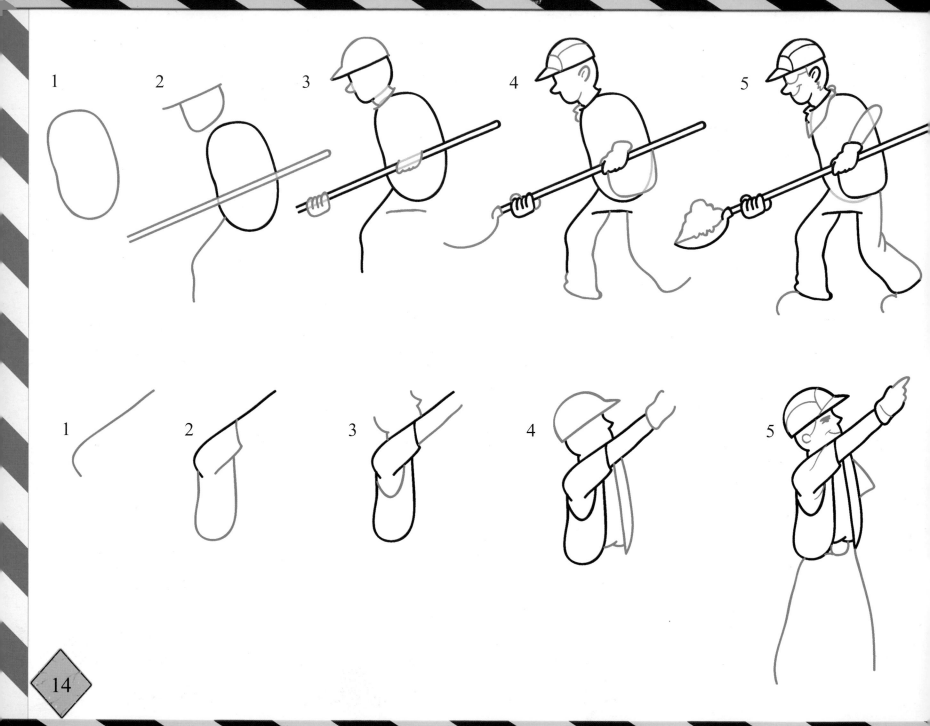

1   2   3   4   5

1   2   3   4   5

On the Construction Site

These pages show some items you might want to include when drawing your construction site.

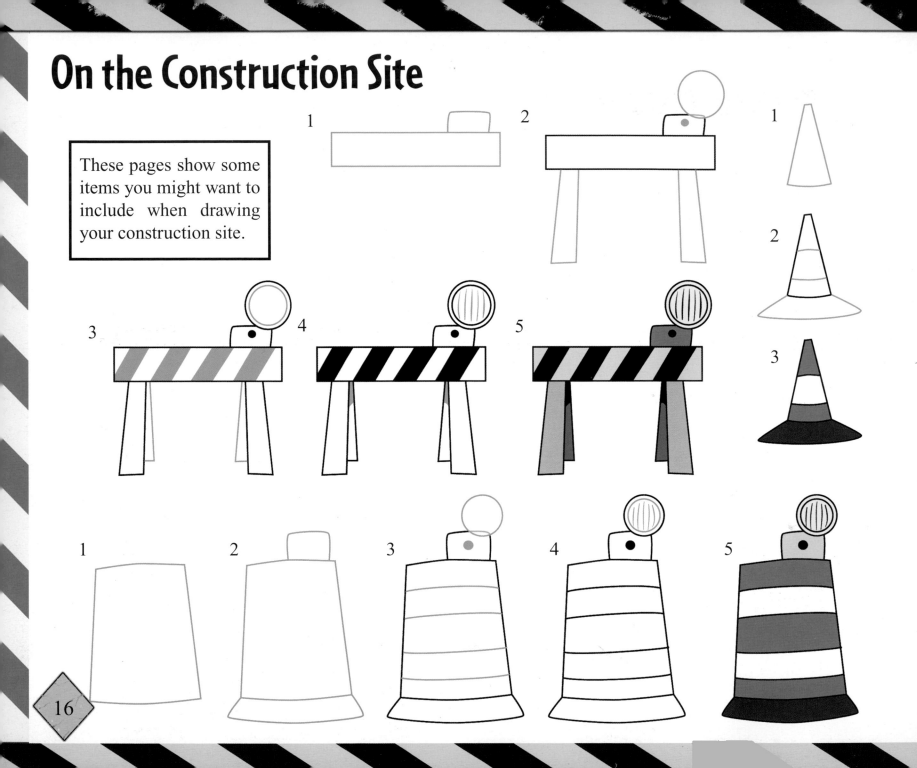

FELLED TIMBER

FILL DIRT

BOULDERS

CONSTRUCTION SIGNS

CAUTION
AREA UNDER CONSTRUCTION

DETOUR →

ROAD CONSTRUCTION AHEAD

Mighty Dump Truck

1

2

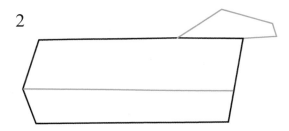

3

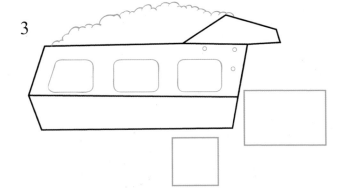

4

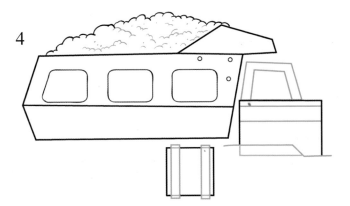

5

6

7

8

Tonka

Mighty Dump Truck Unloading

1

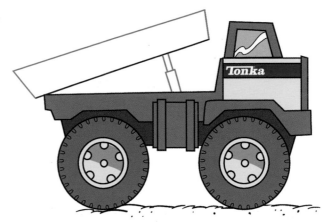

2

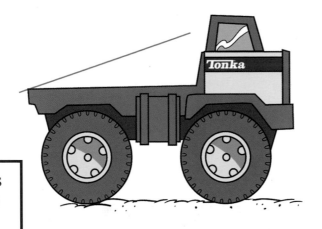

Follow the steps
on pages 18–19
for the body
of the truck.

3

4

5

6

7

21

Mighty Cement Mixer Front

1

2

3

4

5

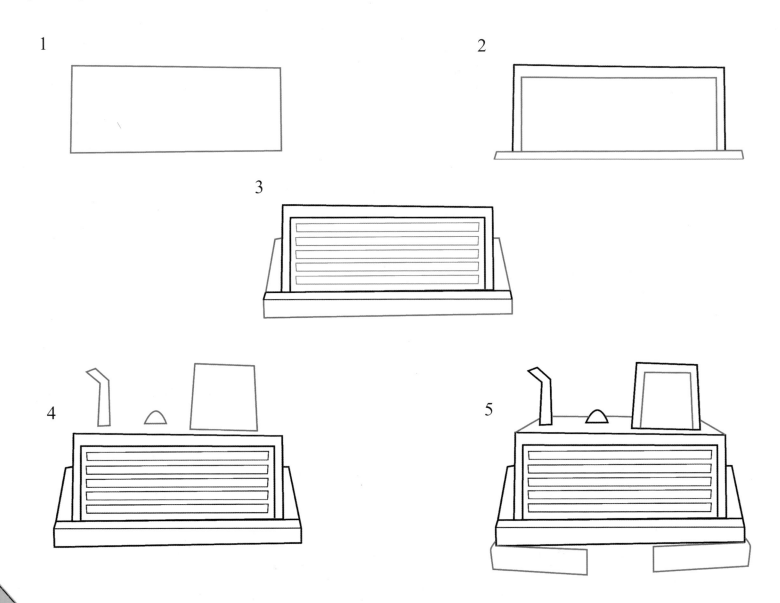

6

7

8

9

23

Mighty Cement Mixer

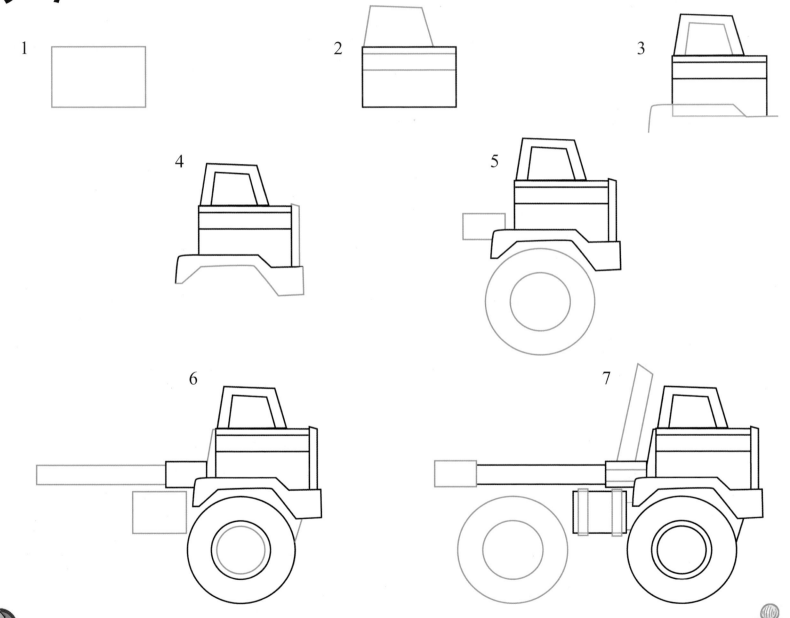

1

2

3

4

5

6

7

24

8

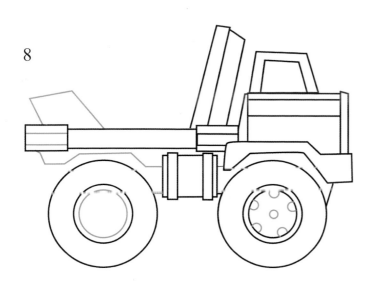

9

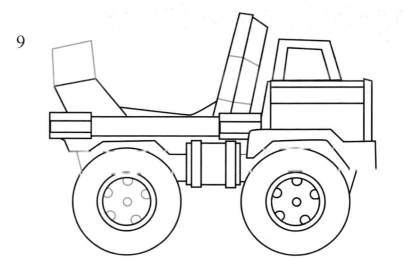

10

11

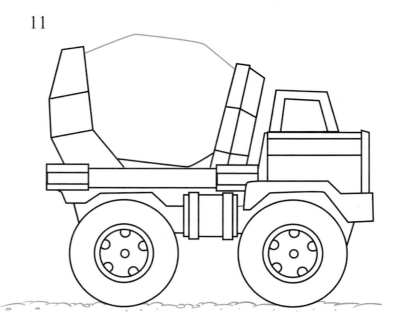

25

12

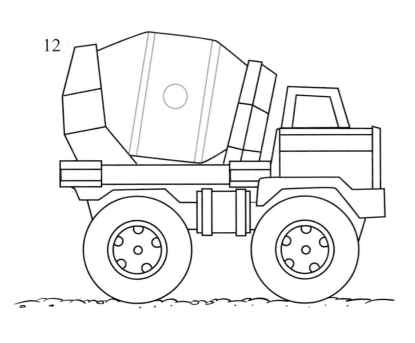

13

14

Tough Grader

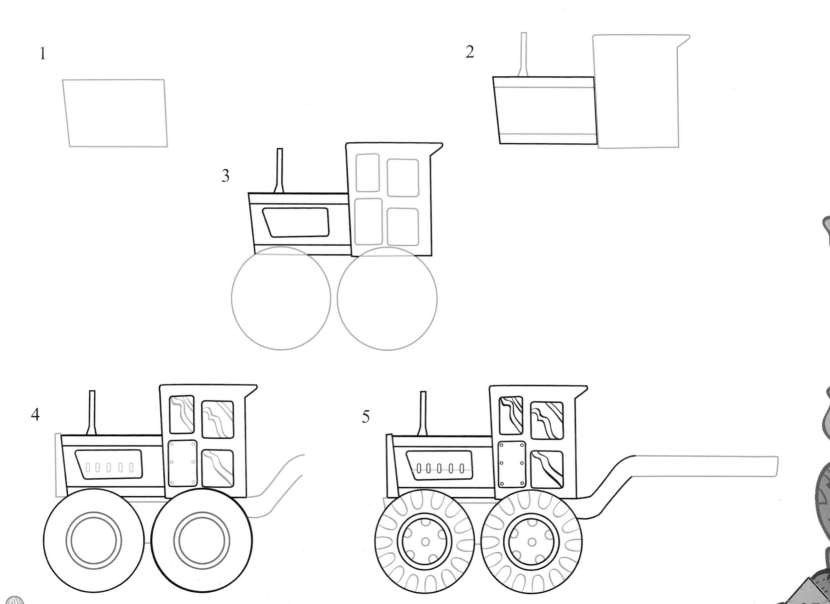

1

2

3

4

5

27

6

7

8

28

9

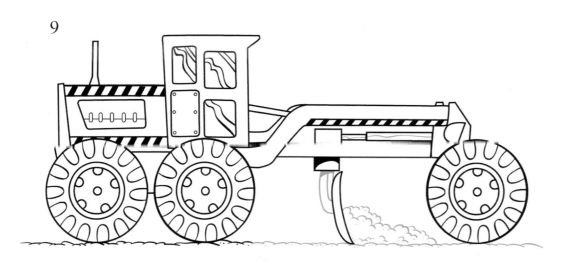

10

Mighty Crane

1

2

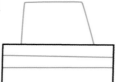

3

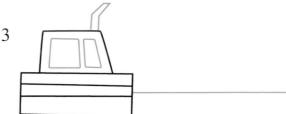

4

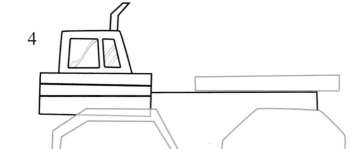

5

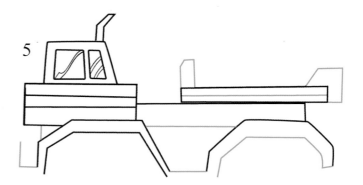

6

7

8

31

9

10

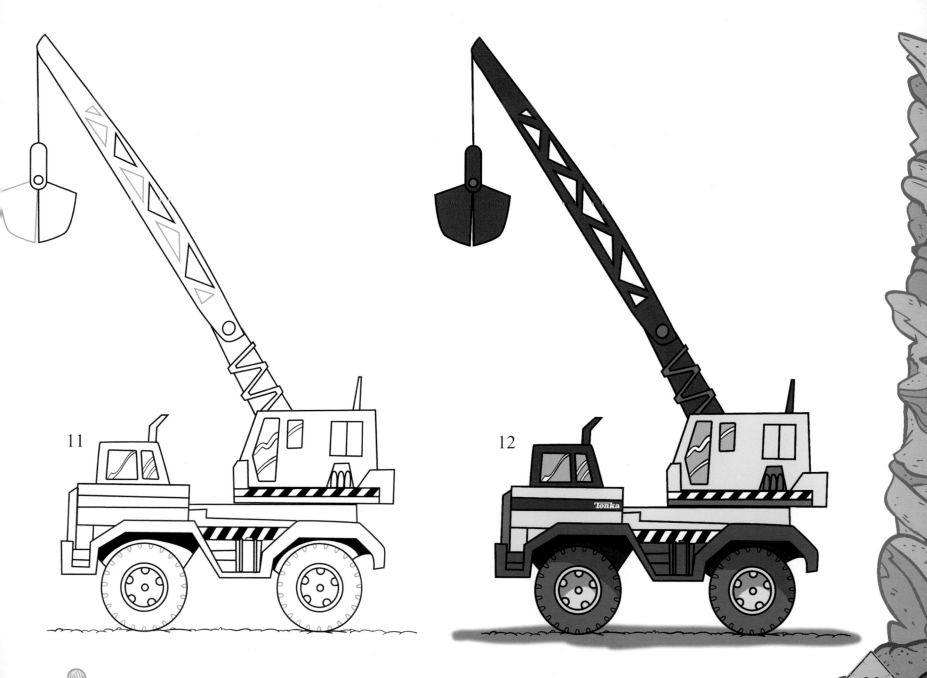

11

12

33

Mighty Backhoe

1

Follow the steps on pages 30–31 for the body of the truck.

2

3

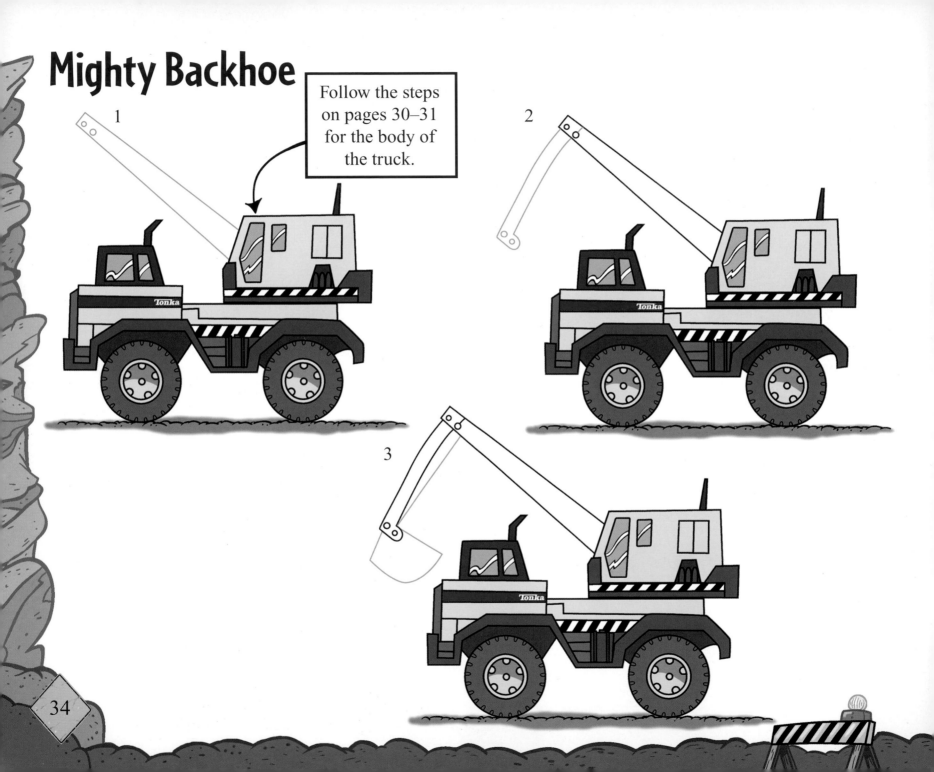

34

4

5

6

35

Mighty Logger

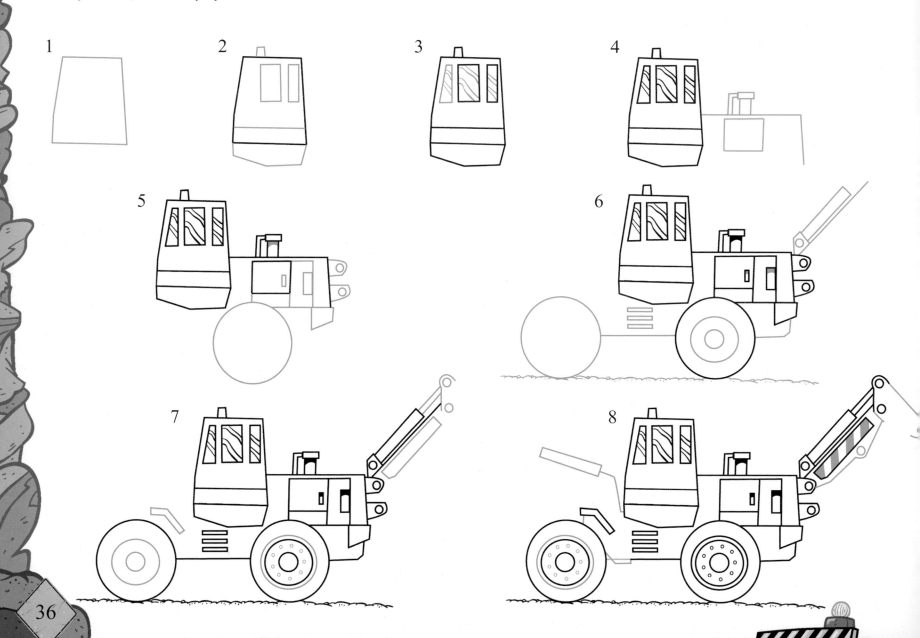

1
2
3
4
5
6
7
8

9

10

11

12

13

14

Tonka

38

Big Rig

1

2

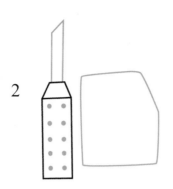

3

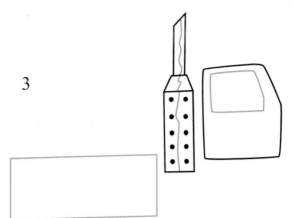

4

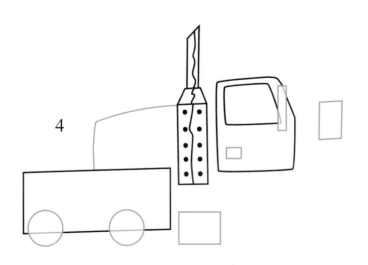

5

39

6

7

8

9

10

11

41

Tough Mighty Crane

1

2
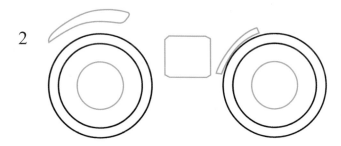

3
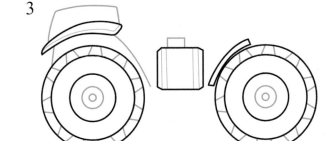

4
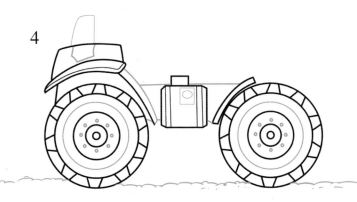

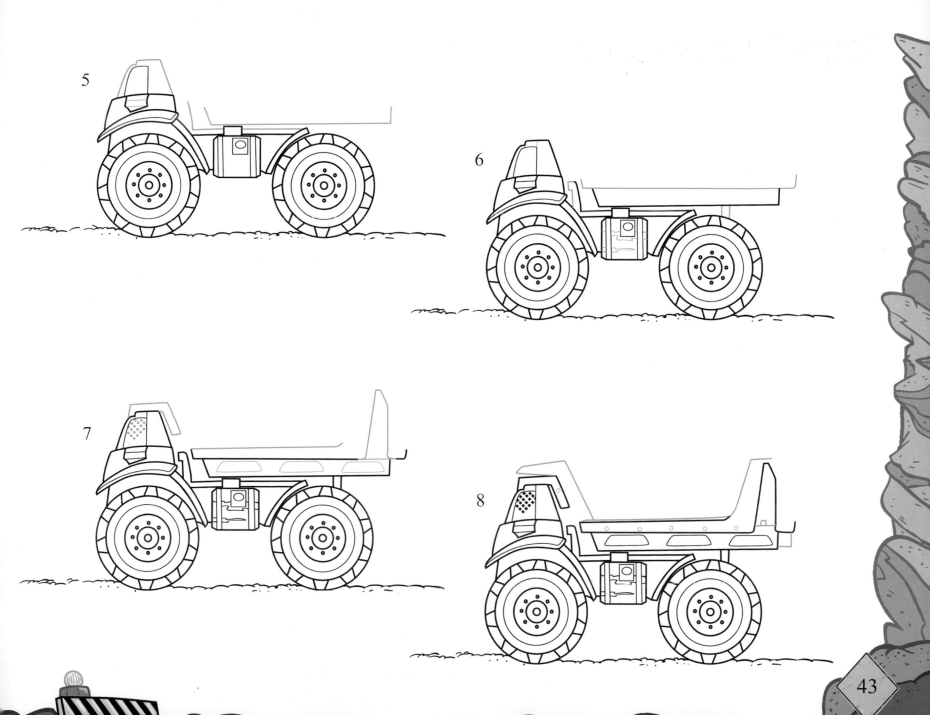

5

6

7

8

43

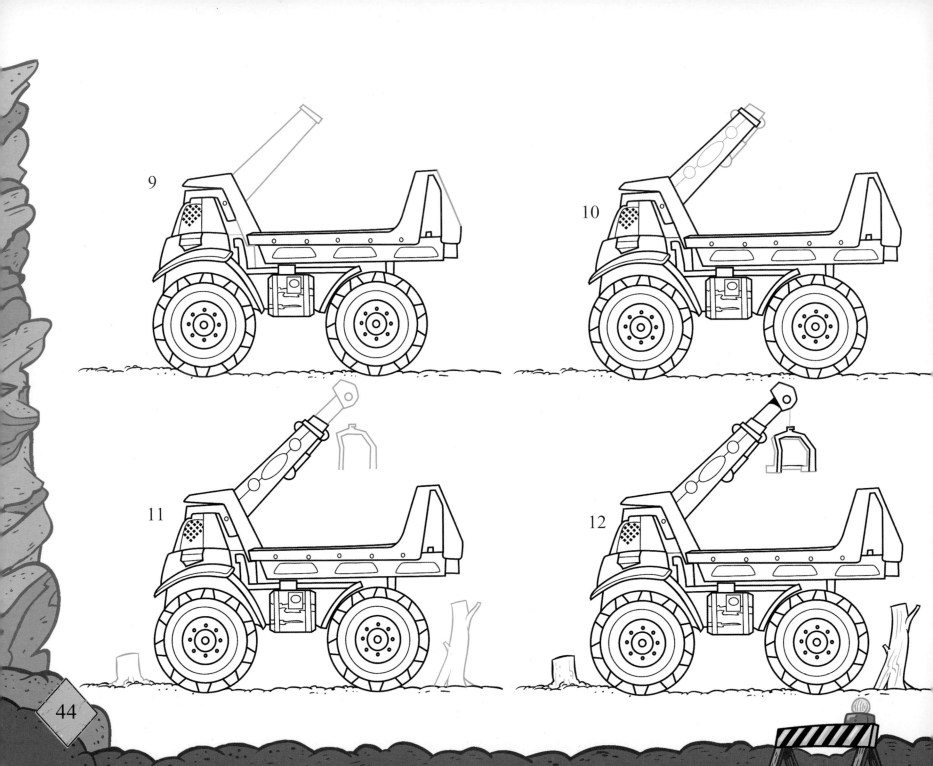

9

10

11

12

13

14

15

16

45

Tough Trencher Backhoe

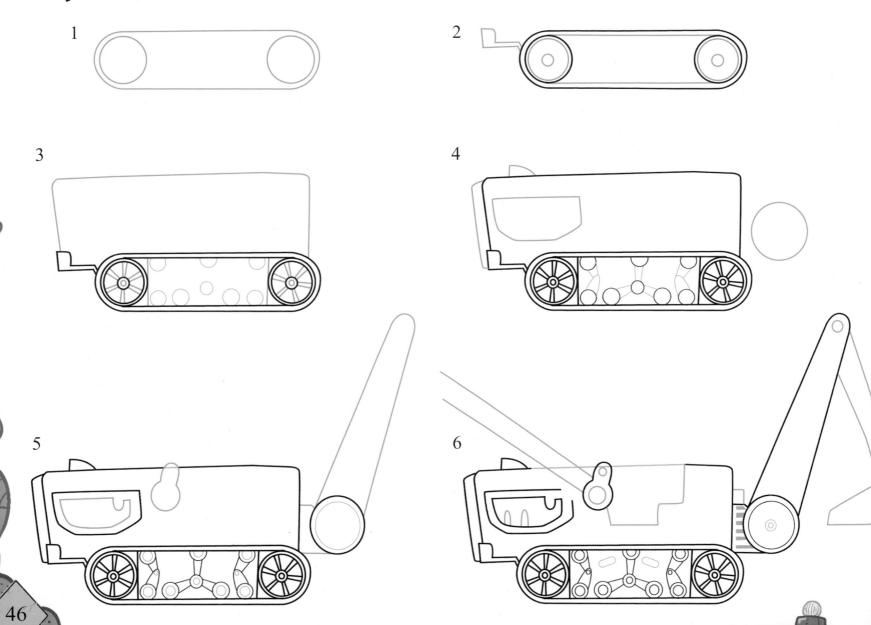

1

2

3

4

5

6

46

7

8

9

10

11

12

Tonka

Mighty Front Loader

1

2

3

4

5

50

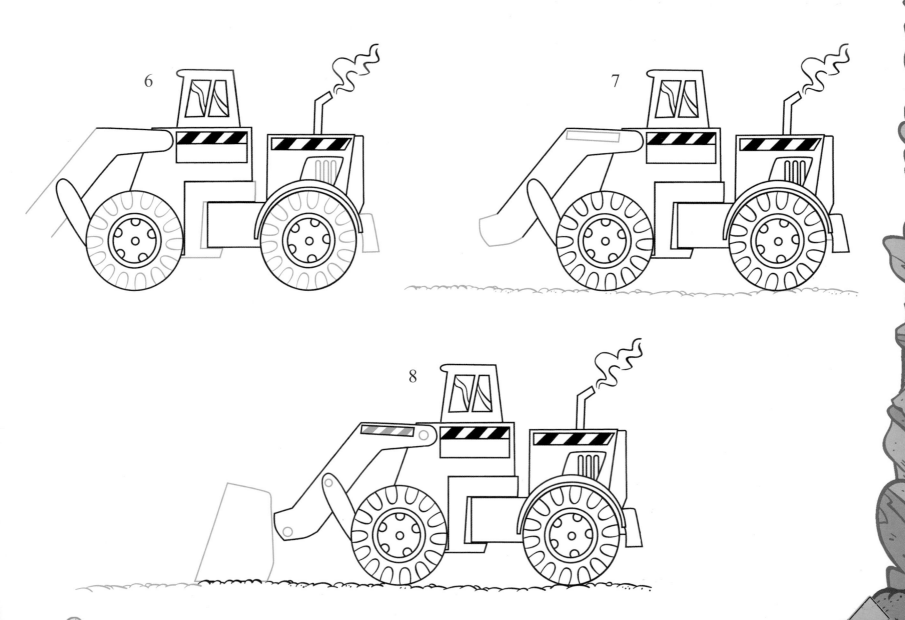

9

10

11

52

Mighty Front Loader Dumping Dirt

1

Follow the steps on pages 50–51 for the body of the truck.

2

3

4

5

6

54

Tough Mighty Front Loader

1
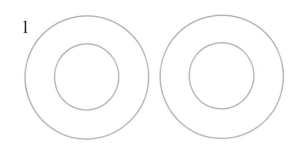

2
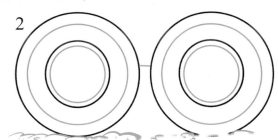

3
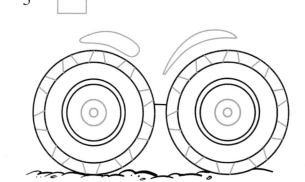

4
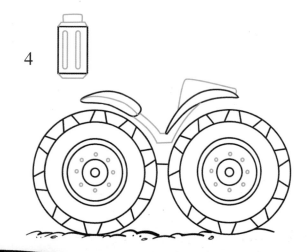

5
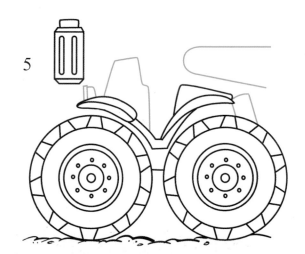

55

6

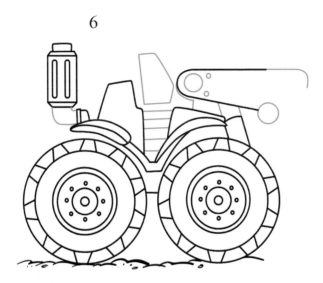

7

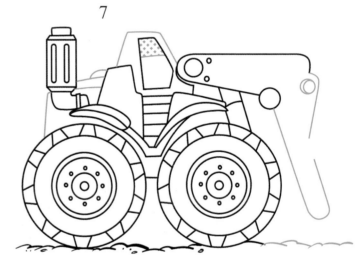

8

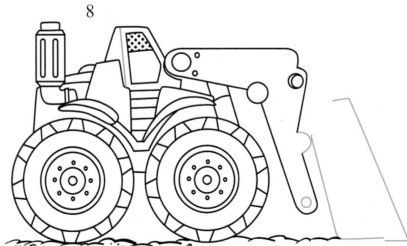

9

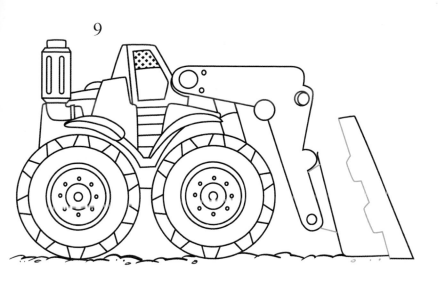

10

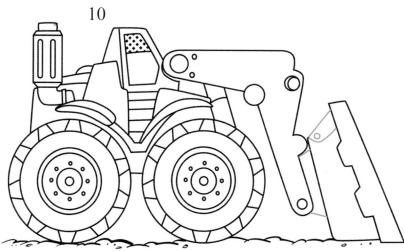

11

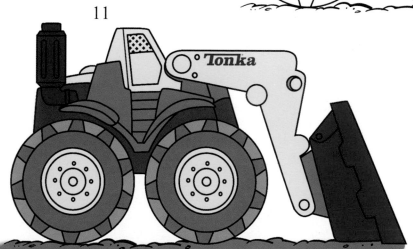

Tough Mighty Road Roller

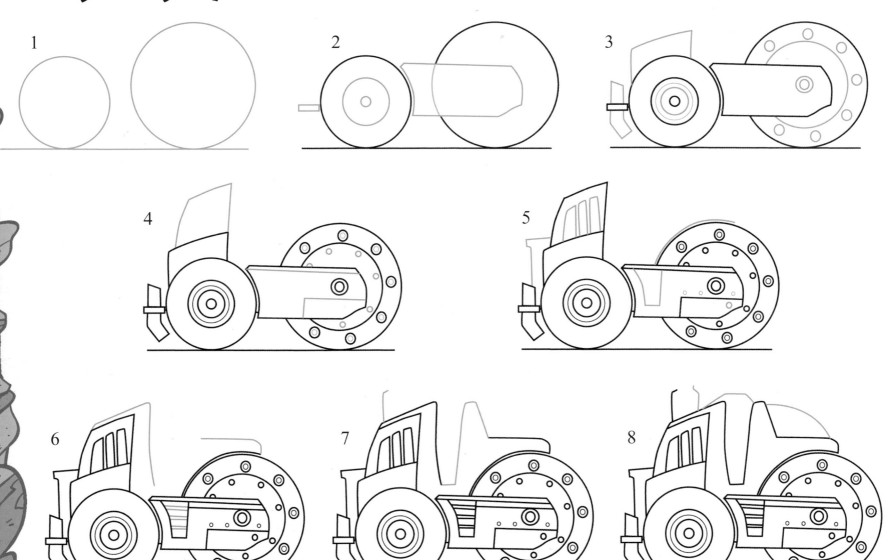

1

2

3

4

5

6

7

8

58

9

10

11

12

13

Tough Quarry Dump

1

2

3

4

5

6

7

60

8

9

10

11

Tonka

61

Tough Quarry Dump Front

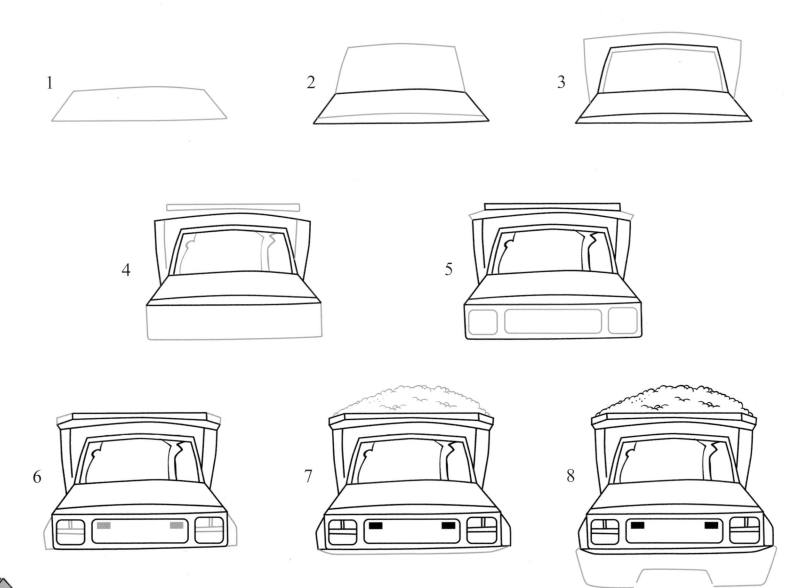

1

2

3

4

5

6

7

8

9

10

11

13

12

63

About the Artist

Steve began drawing in first grade and never stopped. Now he draws for a living, working on all kinds of games and books for children to enjoy. When Steve isn't drawing, he can be found playing with his two goofy dogs or working on his garden. Steve currently lives in Clintonville, Ohio, with his lovely wife Karen and the two goofy dogs.

Other Pencil, Paper, Draw!™ books to look for:

Pencil, Paper, Draw!™
Animals

Pencil, Paper, Draw!™
Dinosaurs

Pencil, Paper, Draw!™
Dogs

Pencil, Paper, Draw!™
Cars and Trucks

Pencil, Paper, Draw!™
Fantasy Creatures

Pencil, Paper, Draw!™
Horses

Pencil, Paper, Draw!™
Pirates

Pencil, Paper, Draw!™
Sharks

Pencil, Paper, Draw!™
Flowers

Pencil, Paper, Draw!™
Baby Animals

Pencil, Paper, Draw!™
Mr. Potato Head™

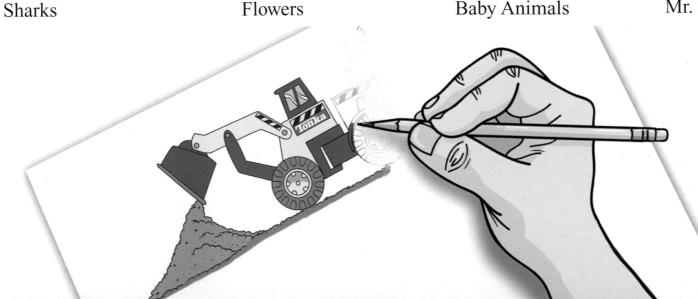